A POET IS A I

SHORT POEMS AIN'T GOT NOBODY TO LOVE

Edited by Raundi Moore-Kondo

For the Love of Words

We believe...

A poet is a poet is a poet
no matter how tall,
and a poem is a poem
no matter how long.

We're not scientists,
but we have a hunch
you will find these pint-sized
pieces really pack a punch.

Some say it is their
low-center of gravity
multiplied by a penchant
for breaking hearts and levity...

With only about 100 words
to create a work of art
there isn't room for anything
more than pure heart.

Short Poems
Ain't Got Nobody
to Love

Ellyn Maybe

Enjoy The World!

If your footsteps mix with a periscope
let's call you a submarine or a dolphin.

If your air sings into the helium of a balloon
let's call you music and leave it at that.

If your mind is part past and part future
let's call you the present.

If your memories stick to your heart like velcro
Let's call you human.

If there's a suitcase dangling on the edge of your life.
Let's call you the world.

Michael Cantin

First Step

When that first amphibian kissed the earth
do you think it looked back towards the sea?

Did it bemoan the loss of being able to dance
in each and every direction?

Or was the discovery of sky too beguiling
as it was wrapped in a blanket of stars?

Was looking back even an option?
Its eyes were perfectly adapted
to a different life.

How terrifying it must have been,
to have to relearn how to see.

Mark Olague

Nightmarch

Things
March against
Us.
Terribly insistent
Things.
We sleep against
Them
& wake
Beneath
Dewy & dreadful
Heels.

Kelsey Bryan-Zwick

Pebble And Tide

My heart
Worn sea glass you palm
As you walk the shores

My want
The way wind curls, is
Felt yet, unseen

The sky
My lungs unfurling
As a well placed sigh

To feel small
Let everything in
Pebble, moon, tide

To feel big
Let the sands loose of
Your grip, grain by grain

My heart
Raw mussel, curved shell
A glimmer in the wrack

Ellen Webre

Alligator Girl

Emeralds in the riverbed
make glass pebbles soft
under webbed feet.
Kisses are stolen
like ripe apricots
in the stream.
Eyes roll yellow
and a tail swishes
through the swamp.
Have you seen her yet?
Long fanged and sweet
with children in her mouth?

Matt Rouse

Belly Flop

Watch this dad
I made up a brand new dive
You've never seen anything like THIS!

Steven Hendrix

Undertow

unseen force, always looking to pull us under
I listen to the rhythm of the water
to prepare for its coming
and brace myself
in the sand,
unstable,
waiting
for the rush
of water, close my eyes
and feel the sensation against
my legs, toes grabbing the sand tight
hoping still to be standing when it passes

Ruth Blue

Tadpoles

The river flows by,
caressing new born tadpoles,
granting them their chance.

Robbi Nester

Tree Frog: A Self-Portrait

The poison arrow frog is small but loud,
throat pumping like a piston, vibrant skin
a warning to all would-be carnivores
that this one bite would be their last.
Born in a tapioca-mass of eggs,
one tiny comma, then borne,
still legless, on a parent's
back to a convenient pool
of rainwater caught between
two broad leaves of a bromeliad..
Seldom seen, this frog
sings for the joy of being heard.

Torrin A. Greathouse

The Sky Fisher

When I hear their chirping
labored by the weight
of the rising sun
I imagine birds
with fishhooks in their beaks.
Made suddenly so aware
of all the gravity in their flights,
and all of their brothers reborn
as cardinals when
the fishermen of
the ground got the best of them.

Thea Iberall

Separation

I loved your shadows once when we were beyond
all longing. I never knew you to be untrue.

Yet when you took to the road that morning, did you
know there was to be no more us, no more winters

Just the endless flurry of unknown breaths,
and the moon darkening the uninterruptable sky?

Eric Morago

Reverse

We were reverse alchemy. Gold
changed back to lead. Our hearts,
a pair of origami cranes, unfolded
paper once again. The language
of goodbye devolved to wordless
gesture—a civil nod, then muted
bodies, backwards-turned. Now
I am fish, grown gills and writhe
to find water, to swim, to dive—
to escape the dirt, the earth, you.

Elizabeth Iannaci

Poem Written On Paper Made From Old Love Letters

I could say it was a day
that woke unweary—
ladled light taking its time
to stretch and be seen,
a day mother to itself
a day like any other. Or

I could say I should have
worried when dogs whispered
to one another in short,
controlled bursts, when
neighbors stopped ticking,
and the hot fusion of
an August calendar froze. Or

I might say it was
a big bang of a day,
an Alamogordo blast of
a day, a cold carcass
or a black hole of a day—
a day like all those
yet to come.

Carlisle Huntington

Wild Heart

I went to the Doctor today.
He told me I have a heart condition.
He showed me shiny blue X-rays,
Of a bird trapped inside a cage,

its wings thrashing,
its voice crying,
begging for release,
but if I let her fly free,
she may very well
be the death of me.
That's what the Doctor said,
at least.

So I kept her locked up
inside of my chest,
the Wild Heart
that cannot be put to rest.

But the wild heart did,
What a wild heart does:
Breaks rib-bone cages
chasing light just because.

Alexis Tan

Caged

Once last month,
I had a bird,
He lived in a cage,
I thought he was always happy,
He had food, drink,
Even toys to play with every day,
I wanted him to sing,
I guess he was never in the mood.

Last week,
I had a bird,
He still lived in a cage,
Every time,
When I walked by,
He would flap his wings,
Calling out,
I suppose he loved me,

Yesterday,
My bird was still there,
He stared at me with his dead, black eyes,
But he was never truly alive.

Sarah ChristianScher

The Year the Sound Came From the Bottom of the Pacific

-from a ghostline by Analise Gellman

I was a child
dressed snugly in coat and boots
sitting sedately on the sand;
contemplating the end of the earth,
and the beginning of infinity.
As the other children ran,
squealing at marooned jellyfish and land-locked algae,
I heard the ocean's roar
humming through my bones like whale-song.

Megan Richtman

The Ancient Whale

Clouds navigate an ocean of astral pinpoints, coiling
in sharp winds.
Observing the needle of an azimuth compass,
they chart their course across the constellations.
Below, the prehistoric seabed litters the sands with
shells of creatures
from ages long ago.

Remains of crustaceans and mollusks
coral and cuttlefish beaks
lie unperturbed beneath the dunes.
Air filled with the briny perfume of
the Mediterranean
toss sand across an old skeleton.

A beetle scuttles across mountains of vertebrae
into the crevasses of the forgotten skull.
Thirty-five million years it had lain there,
a shadow on the seabed
a ghost in the Sahara.

Steven Hendrix

Layers of Thirst and Dust

my mother used to
recite a popular nursery rhyme
on rainy days during my childhood

rain, rain go away
come back another day
little Steven wants to play

and it worked
the rain has mostly stayed away
for thirty years now
and memory thirsts for those childhood days
of sitting, staring out the window
with an intense longing to play
a feeling unknown now
like a forgotten dream

work has piled on over the years
like the layers of dirt and dust
waiting to be washed away
and the longing now is for the rain
with a burgeoning desire to play in it

Kelsey Bryan-Zwick

Midwest Summer Bluegrass

The swap water
the lotus, the green
algae sludge of mud slick
off sleek rain boots

The frogs bloom as the
warm, salt-humid winds roll in
smell of rain clouds gathering

The husky tall length of grass
dandelion dander tufts
whippoorwills and cattails
a hollow gust through the reeds

There is a music
it takes lonesome ears to hear
in the echo's of rushing water
the prism and fleck
of backcountry river inlets

Canelle Irmas

Water Spider

This long-legged water spider, thin, small,
wisp the color of dust,
has his legs splayed wide
over the lake, making
dents in the cool covering sheen,
the reflection of its body upside down
under it. he skips
over flexing mouths of fish who look
almost like they're breathing,
struggling for breath,
tilted sideways to see,
with one huge, slow-blinking eye,
a little spider perched over their sky.

John Gardiner

Coyote

Coyote in the canyon faces me
soaked through at 5 A.M.
and in no mood to retreat
back to where the storm
breeds thunder and gathers lightning
for fresh assaults.
Coyote gathers resolve
and looks at me
as if I were the fool
I've often thought myself to be.
After all, what particular and lucid
excuse can I make,
just as wet as coyote
and crossing uninvited through his yard.

Ruth Blue

Thunder

Pearly Lightning,
booming thunder startling,
stark black skies.
Moments of utter calmness,
inside the raging storm.

Jaimes Palacio

Possible

Water falls
seeds the
possible.

Robin Dawn Hudechek

Night Rose

Petals sweat in moonlight
as darkness pools on the ground,
veins curling like eyelashes
fixed on an empty sky

Daniel McGinn

Almost Eden

A fresh flower
in its chilled cup
stares unblinking at the morning

Warm dew quivers
like teardrops
atop the slick leaves

A snail dragging spirals on its back
presses its belly
against the green stem

Birds gather
like tiny angels singing
in the first light

A.D. Winans

Rain Poem

the rain beats a rhythm against
the windshield
the wipers flail helplessly
like a fish out of water
demons to the left of me
demons to the right of me
demons in front of me
demons in back of me

my brain a barbecue pit
feeds on the rolling thunder
spits out bits and pieces of poems
words of emptiness words of despair
shadow creatures lay mutilated
in nearby ditches

a Highway Patrol car speeds past me
its red light flashing
the sky black as a groom's tuxedo

Cynthia Quevedo

Blast Of Spring

  Happy moss
glows green   amid
  small pebbles
surrounded by slabs
   of gray slate

Cynthia Quevedo

Rain

beats
dying
leaves off
branches
building
a pile of gold
at the base of the trunk.

A.D. Winans

Li Po

he sat beneath the trees
talking to the leaves
wine flowed into miniature glasses
of silent sound
intoxicated on its flavor
he tasted it like a brew master
gazed at the sky
spoke a poet's dialogue
to the passing clouds
the red wine flowing
through his veins

Marie Lecrivain

"i can't even…"

i long to write a poem
that wouldn't offend anyone
with words that inspire
kind talk and accolades
revolution and sunsets
without barbs that wend
their way into the minds
of the over-fatigued
who want to burn flags
films and all poems
written and unwritten
but that's not my job
as an imperfect seer
with bifurcated vision
and a heart heavy
with the weight
of a world gone dark
with cruel indifference

Steven Hendrix

Basquiat: Untitled (Life Study), 1983

the things we carry:
wax wings
melting

I am the sum of my parts
seen and unseen
and subtracted

I am less than my eyes see
I am more than your eyes see

do not dissect me
or create your maps upon me
or think that you can discover me
when I haven't yet discovered myself

Jaimes Palacio

Self Portrait In Charcoal

shadows in my blood
i am nothing
less than smoke

Torrin A. Greathouse

For The Ghost Of Van Gogh's Ear

Do you wonder if he blamed you for every whisper?
Twists of ochre and turpentine in the wind,
that fell like pirouetting clouds into you?

Fool—bursting violets clenched like fists.

Madman—cerulean window shards.

Freak—a shade of black your hands had never dared
to mix.

Does it burn your tender shriveled skin,
still, to think he believed
your life had more meaning in its part
than as part of the whole?

That you could not hear his final words
whispered before giving you away,
wrapped in ivory and rust like a precious gift?

"Guard this object carefully."

Deanne Meeks Brown

Open

I folded in on myself
Like an envelope

Sealed tight
With hand of the Queen Wax Stamp

An ordinary letter opener
Would not do

It took a sharp blade
To break the seal
And pour my contents out

Dani Neiley

benign

When wishing on stars didn't cut it anymore and you ran out of eyelashes I went down to the pond behind our neighborhood on August afternoons, started skipping stones. The high school got their dissection frogs from the rocky shore: pumped the bodies full of formaldehyde, stretched them flat on tin pans, and I thought about you, unconscious on an operating table. So I closed my eyes, palmed smooth pebbles in my hand, threw them as far as I could. The stones only stayed on top for so long, you see. The sinking was all too familiar.

Canelle Irmas

There Is Beauty In A Broken Watch

There is beauty in a broken watch,
its slim hands bent beyond telling,
that does not know the time.
Something precious in its cracked glass,
metal casing scratched and used,
springs and gears spilling out the back.
It would be a shame to fix it
even if you could,
to rob it of its shattered charm.
Better to stay and see the unfunctional pieces
And hear the absence of its *tick*
                              tock
              tick
                              tock

Matt Rouse

A Useful Thing

He was cleaning out the shop
Before the move
When he came across an odd object
In a pile of metal
On a shelf
In the corner
He picked it up
And rolled it through
His dirt greased fingers
It was black
Shaped in a T
Tapered at the end
Into a hexagon
He could not remember what it did
Or where it came from
He didn't even know
If it was a tool
Or a part to some larger machine
He smiled at it
Then took it from the pile

And put it into his pocket

Sorting The Trash

I have this weird thing about waste
        I can't throw away paper that I no longer need,
so I do math equations on them
        Until they are no longer waste paper, but papers
ready for trash.

I track how long it takes me to do homework with a
stopwatch
If I take too much time to write a poem, I abandon it
And that, in itself, is a waste.

funny

The nights that I spend anxiously wondering if you
loved me -
In my mind, those nights are not waste.
Simply exercises in patience

Carlisle Huntington

On Shaving

I didn't shave my legs today.
I didn't see the point
trying to appear anything more
 than Human,

In stripping my hide,
like a hunter strips an elk,
sanding myself down,
drying myself out
Like your new leather wallet,
So I can hold your identity,
Your money,
Your pictures,
But still somehow belong to you.

I didn't shave my legs today.
I didn't see the point.
trying to appear anything less than
a Woman,
Not smooth like a baby,
Clinging,
And crying.

I didn't shave my legs today.
It's a small gesture,
But it's mine.

Elizabeth Iannaci

Fourth Floor Terrace

dove gray sky sliding
into dove gray flagstones,
breathing in my 20 minutes—
inhaling grilled cheddar and
avocado with French fries
while my arteries harden.
If I were Frank O'Hara
I'd say the traffic sounds
like 700 Lana Turners
fleeing photographers.
If I were Frank O'Hara
I'd have a Scotch in my hand,
I'd write more, eat sardines,
appreciate primary colors,
watch out for dune buggies.

Heather Noel Aldridge

Plastered In Paris

Little old me Sitting by the sea
Ferocious hole Where you used to be
It's not over until it's over'd
So why do we pretend to be unaffected and calloused?
The skin has visibly grown over.
The fangs affixed, the fists protectively clenched
The wall, unconsciously in place.
When still, I would positively crumble
If you, just for old times sake
Tell that it meant something
More than this

Trista Hurley-Waxali

A Drawer Find

The hotel bible had
an inscription:

To those in need,
take this home.

Thomas R. Thomas

touch the pages
spill your coffee on them
put your DNA in

The book will be part of you
become one with the author

Richard Nester

What One Gets Eventually
for Helen Rivera

One nice thing about Paris is that it stays put.
You've visited enough to know this and remark on it.
Stepping from "a motor" outside the Hotel de
Crillon in 1909,
Edith Wharton spots the first "aeroplane" to
cross a city,
while you standing in virtually the same spot
and looking in the same direction see nothing
miraculous,
the ordinary sun crossing an ordinary sky,
which on this
one day, much later, is miracle enough for you.

Eric Lawson

Autumn Hue

The window frames
a perfect portrait of
fall's decent upon the
sleepy hamlet of lost
childhood's domain

Betsy Mars

Apple Picking

Sorting through trees heavy with ripeness,
ripe with heaviness.
Apples cling fleetingly, chosen or left to rot.
Foreign varieties hitherto strange and so distrusted.
Rejecting the bruised, the awkward,
the easily-plucked low-hanging fruit
for something idealized -
the fabled fruit of Snow White fame,
glistening, tempting, flawless.
Yet lacking a poison core. Seedless.
Holding out for perfection,
thin-skinned,
slighting the mottled, mangled, or misshapen
in the Garden of Eden in her virginal heart.

Emma Morrison

Sitting

I sit high up in a tree
Waiting for the mist to clear
And the sun to rise above the forest trees

As the mist clears
I climb down and set my two feet
carefully on the ground

Leaves crunch under
the pressure of my toes
As I set back for home

Canelle Irmas

The Setting Light

The sun doesn't always set in the rainforest.
Most of the time the clouds are so thick
with water that the sky is not blue
but a cold, grey skin overhead. I sit
on a concrete back porch, my feet
in the jungle's grass, my face in
the jungle's wet air, watching
the sky slip away.
For hours,
I look as far as my eyes
can reach to see the clouds go slow
into the dark. The tree line starts to fade
behind the hours. Everything dims.
There are no vibrant colors, only
the light fading, closing
like a hand.

Mari Maxwell

My Malaysian Friend

On Coral Beach where the aquamarine waters trickle
we sat and yapped.
Supped coffee from your flask and ate
okra, curry chicken and Jasmine rice.
You read to me words of love, of ardour,
your latest poetry.

I'm smiling again at the roll of your tongue,
sultry in mid-afternoon sunshine.
Undressing each word - like the coral sanding
our skin to smoothness.
Basking in moments of joy
and friendship.
As time and summer linger -
over Cafe Au Lait and Connemara Coral.

Micah Kunkle

A Day

A day. One last day.
To go and play,
At Catalina.
We had so much fun
playing in a pit, and in the sun.
But it's my last day.
My one last day. To go and play.
At Catalina

Cindy Rinne

Today I Got Invited To Visit India

Your elephant necklace looks like it is from India. Would you like to go with me? I am purchasing airplane tickets soon. You can stay at my home. Experience the land of contrasts. Last time I was there I picked up a wooden Buddha and on the bottom the label said, 'Made in China.' Imagine that! The food is different from north to south and to the coast. And the fabrics, beautiful. December and January are the best times to visit. The summer is too hot, she says.

Linda Singer

Summer 2015

Cooking-frying-mean-heat,
punches-in-the-stomach-heat,
reflects from the sidewalk,
can't-hide-in-the-dark-enough-heat,
windows covered in black cardboard,
gasp-for-air-eyes-water-ears-stopped-up-heat.

An angel on my shoulder, wilted puddle,
whispers in my ear, this is what hell is like,
just like this, burning-up-the-wall-heat.

Where is the ice, a little rain will do,
I will accept the smallest drizzle heat.
Devil on my shoulder, it's only a drought,

not end of the world,

not global warming,

wait,

maybe it is

just

that

heat.

Seth Halbeisen

Important Notes on Proper Table Manners

"Secretly--on the inside--I'm kind of dying"
Seth Halbeisen

Anything that slows the acquisition
of food is an implement.
This why I hate salad forks,
or wonder why serving spoons
are too large for my mouth.
I think it's safe to say
one should never eat with a spatula.
God knows I have tried.
The five second rule is only enforced
if your mother-in-law is present.
Elbows on the table
are a sure sign
that your guests did not like the appetizers,
or in certain circumstances,
the lack of proper side dishes.

Sheri Black-Flynn

Wine Stain

Merlot splash on my carpet
Company stayed too long
Dirty dishes in the sink
Midnight! Was that the 12th gong?

My tired body crawls into bed
The pillow quiets my brain
I shoot up, eyes wide open
I forgot to clean the stain!

Glen Nesbitt

Soap

She says she's cooking soap.
Another night of chicken noodle soap.
Wash it down with a glass of suds.
The pot is not necessarily hot just because it bubbles.
She says she's cooking soap.
Another day of Irish Spring Stew.
Her spaghetti's the best.
She cooks it up with zest.
Baby, I love your soap so $%&* much.
Yeah, I cussed. What are you going to do?
Wash my mouth out with soap?
I already ate.
The best thing about cooking soap is
You don't have to wash the dishes.

Aryanna Miramontes

If Bubbles Were Bullets

If bubbles were bullets, I'd take
a shot for you. If bubbles were
bullets, I'd blow them out for you.
If bubbles were bullets, I'd
pop them out for you.
If bubbles were bullets, I'd do
anything for you.

Rachel Foster

chores

the breadcrumbs sit
on the counter,
waiting
turning stale,
getting harder.

they are swept away,
tossed
to the floor
to make the kitchen appear
clean.

the ants come
in and conquer.
moving the debris.
the little soldiers
carry their own weight.

they work together,
each building,
pushing
the next one
further.

the marching stops.
a Lilliputian trainwreck –

the catastrophic
end,

only temporary.

together, they regain themselves.
one carries a heavier load –
does not toss the fallen

to the kitchen floor
to become stale
he takes
on the burden:
carries the wounded,
the hardened,
and himself.

Briceida Campana

BFF

Me and you are friends.
You smile, I smile.
You're hurt, I'm hurt.
You cry, I cry.
You jump of a bridge,
 I'm goanna miss you.

CHANGING PERCEPTION IS POSSIBLE

It's that long fall off a short ladder.

Aryanna Miramontes

The Regret Ride

Woosh!
Down it goes.
So fast it lasts one blink.

Screaming is the only sound.
All of a sudden! Screech!
A stop.

So high above the ground
It looks like the opening
Doors of heaven.

But then, a slight move
And here we go on
Another ride.

Vanessa Barrera

Rollercoaster

Step into the car
A stomach flutter
A thought of regret
the bar comes down
with a thump

the climb starts its way
up up up in the sky
creaking while climbing

Silent pause..........
AHHHHH!!!!!
over the hills we go
with a crack and
whoosh accelerating
down down down with
pure screaming turns
and drops nonstop then a
rest,

Tick tick tick the climb
starts again a heart flutter
in one breath we dive
Into the curve sideways
upside down whirling then
back down
the wheels screeching to
A stop

Bryan Gonzalez

The Bicycle Ride

Hands sweating as I gripped onto the handle bars,
In the middle of the road,
The cars beeping and honking,
As my cousin's scooter went "broom",
Then I looked up and I saw the finish line up ahead,
"Bump, bump" I went,
"Chirp, chirp" went a bird,
"Bark" went a dog,
"Hey" said my friend,
"Whoosh" I went,
As I won the race

Darryl Henry

Go Carts

The wind blowing in my face
WHOOSH WHOOSH

WHOOSH racers drifting
Eeerrrhhh rubber burning
In flames smoke filling the
sky
monstrous faces staring
at me until the final lap I
win

first place

Sophia Larsen

Ten is Approaching

Ten is coming, approaching swiftly,
On that special day, January twenty-sixth.
But first I have to get through Christmas,
which is only 15 days, 10 hours,
7 minutes, and 54 seconds away!
(Not that I'm counting.)
On that fatal day,
26th day of the first month,
I will be a two-digit number.
Not sure to be excited or scared,
Shivering and smiling all at once.
But the question is:
Ten – victim or suspect?
Ten – good or bad?
Now, 11 is coming up next!

Daniel McGinn

Growing up
is breaking the horse
the heart rode in on

HanaLena Fennel

The Blue Truck, Twisted House

There was a dream I had as a child
A blue truck carried you away from the driveway
It was early morning, everything was sharp lines and
blue shaded
There was no room for you in the cab
You huddled in the truck bed, bouncing and
cold

There was a dream I had before I knew the truck
was real

The road swung into curves
Throwing you airborne for heartbeats at a time
Winding your terror up the mountain to a
twisted house
I am small, slide both arms into your belt loop
and hug tight
Swing with the work tools

Robbi Nester

Under the Ironing Machine

It fills up nearly half the kitchen,
this rectangular monstrosity, at which
my mother sits, patient, in her chair,
feeding it sheets damp from the washer.
I squat underneath, my skinny knees
hugging my sides, the warm cotton
billowing, a tent where I sit
with my books and sketch pad,
singing to myself.
The sun finds me here,
and I feel all this will last forever,
even after the smooth sheets
lie folded into squares in the basket,
and my mother stands at the counter,
kneading raw egg into hamburger,
offering me a bit on the tip of one finger,
even after the sun sags beneath the sill
and the moon opens her round silver eye.

Warren Allen

Waiting in Line

The child's... balloon...
can't cover, can't... quite cover...
The moon... it's huge...
It hovers, and... uncovers...
A sad reply...
They're saying, and... they're waving...
Goodbye.

The child's room...
It's shuttered, and... it smothers...
the carefree tune
He shudders, and... he wonders...
how gray... could turn... to
green parrots, and... blue swimming pool...
skies.

The child's in tune...
with mothers... and with lovers...
Who pass... him by
They're laughing, and... they're happy...
to wave... and smile
They're playing, and... he's saving, and...
He's waiting...
in line.

Alexis Tan

Teddy Bear

They hear,
They don't judge
Every day, even when I scream or cry,
They never react,
They are my friends,
I don't know what I am to them,
Do they even know?
I pretend they care,
That they aren't just corpses at a eulogy,
Or faraway souls, never to tell a word.
At least I can trust them to my deepest secrets,
They won't tell,
Or are they just silently laughing at my every futile
effort,
Do they sneer when I cry into their shoulders,
I know they have no brain,
But do they have a heart?

Emaan Sheikh

My Toy Penguin

A soft fluffy friend
A toy full of fur
A squishy blue, purple and white rainbow
A beak sharp as an arrow
Long strong flippers
A Snowflake fountain of fun
A blazing happy face
Eyes hard as dice

Terry McCarty

A Visit To The Doctor

the office smelled of disinfectant
and Dr. Fish spoke like Alfred Hitchcock
which scared me
and made me cry
when I slowly pulled down my pants
to prepare for the long hard jab
of the hypodermic needle
as I thought of the candy
I'd get from the admissions nurse
as a consolation prize
for missing Cosmo the Clown
on Channel 6

Betsy Kenoff-Boyd

Kid vs. Adult Prayers

God, let me have red hair like Pippi and find out where the gypsies are that left me with these bogus parents. God, let me be a veterinarian or a belly dancer. Help me find the treasure in the hole en route to China.

Goddess, thanks for weekends. Thank you for my parents. Thanks for letting me enjoy teaching some students to laugh @ English. Goddess, thanks for this wondrous son.

Goddess, please let me write & do yoga. Let me find kisses along the way. Champagne & a dance with everyone would be delightful.

Ellyn Maybe

He's a Handful

He's a handful

Childhood hands you a lemon meringue moment
And aprons are in scarce supply.

I'm a handful.
Adolescence wrote in crayons all over my hopscotch
patterns.
Till reaping and sowing was an arts and craftsman's
house I dwelled in.

The world is full of hands and feet.
Of Clay that never dries,
The World is moist at most.

Always dangling its dreams up to the knees.
Rivers parting like a volcano once lived here.

And it did.

Warren Allen

Scraps

Scraps... It's all their mums could feed into the
Traps.... of hungry little urchins on their
Laps.... but still these scrappy children gained and
Growed.... till they were huge, and then they hit
the road.

Scraps... Their fists were flying faster than their
Yaps... which spewed invective in between the
Slaps... These brawling kids were learning as they
Went... There's what is said, and then there's what is
meant

Anthony Fitzgerald

What You Were and What I Am:

You were the flowers and the grass,
The fresh piece of paper.

You were the view from the mountaintop,
And the autumn colors below.

You were the bright bow of the ship,
Until it sank, sank, sank.

Now I am the lonely night watch,
The old, weathered barn.

Now I am the trashed plastic bag,
And the ghost town it blows through.

Now I am the house after the hurricane,
The broken pencil.

Mark Olague

Object Study

Smudges mark failed grips;
Blurry side reflections film
Grays days teeming outside.
Crowning an oak table,
A rind of sweat
Soaks cherry-dark wood beneath.
Coffee puddles to the bottom
Quickly losing heat
By every emptying hour.
No longer sipped or savored
Or even stirred.
Left well-enough
Alone, coffee ponders undeterred:
To be cold.

Betsy Mars

Black Hole

for my father, 02/21/27-08/12/15

Early dusk as wildfires consume the hillsides.
Smoke signals darken the sky
spreading ashy breath across the land,
Parched—

Heading home to see
my father, clouded lungs fight
for air, darken his mind, signals crossed.
Oxygen deprived, at a loss.
Memories and fears unleashed
from the shadowy corners
of his drug-addled, rattled mind
entrenched.
Parched cells unquenched.
Seeking a rod divine to detect
the infinite passageways to his sanity.

We both struggle to find balance,
trapped in a strange town
under the flickering machine light
tracking his dwindling vitality.

Graham Smith

taking baby steps

taking baby steps
at the beginning, and end,
of a life's journey

Amber Douglas

Placebo Effect

They've Come For The Breadcrumbs And Sour
Grapes
Silently watching you breathing, hovering above you
just before you
awake
they are thus the last weeks lasting well beyond a year
they've come for the symbol of soul sickness
choking you with never been fathomed fears
watching you watch the safe distance disappear
electrifying buttons erasing fingertips
gongs no longer bang with technicolor rave
links lingering festivals forgetting our conscience
borders bold & brave
they have sucker punched ear drums silencing us
from ever becoming
Awake

Jennifer Bradpiece

Afternoon

Day pulls away, shadow arms stretching toward light.

Dusk, a shadow-mime mocking meager
accomplishments,

points sunlit shards onto piles of unopened books,

steak-stained pans, the leftover drippings of
congealed ambition,

stiff like the clock's face in it's five-past-four sneer.

Day collapses onto the couch, eases into the corner
cushions

like an old dog desperate in its final hours,

haunches kicking, fetid tongue licking at its gut

as the room darkens in around its eyes.

Graham Smith

he turned on the lights
so that he would no longer see
what he feared the most

John Gardiner

Loneliness

Loneliness is much colder
than winter's bloated coat
of ice
hanging on the stable door
in the far corner
of the old pasture
where no one goes
any more.

Vaughan Risher

Epiphany

Moments pass

To truly appreciate them
we must realize their existence

We must acknowledge that
our time in this world is finite

We must make a presence in our minds
of the present

If we hold on to that great sea of the past
we won't appreciate

that truly remarkable

and irreplaceable

sense of

being there

Fatima Shaikh

Nature's Flowers

I see small white flowers
The large tall trees and soft grass
I smell flowers very sweet
I feel dandelions.
I hear cool wind wishing through the blue sky
I wonder if there is more nature to explore

Eric Lawson

The Rose Near Broadway & 3rd

Your very existence defies explanation.
You jut up through the cracked cement
like a miniature sequoia, all majestic pride.
You make me pause mid-stride, awed.

How did you get here, oh mighty rose?
Were you seeded from the back of a
long-distance flatbed, who's weary
driver took a turn too sharply, daydreaming
about dalliances with Southern Belles?

How did you last here, sprightly upstart?
Were you secretly nourished by loving
shop owners who had no gardens of
their own; so in turn they adopted you,
your cause their own vicarious mission?

I pause to take a picture but am jostled.
I take a snapshot with my mind instead.
I move closer to the Bradbury, then turn
and witness a gloved hand snatch you away

Ralph R. Moore

The Illusive Factor

If there's no one you love in this broad land,
Just go to the beach and play in the sand.

Take a handful and put it near your heart,
Feel it penetrate like a Cupid's dart.

Now look around and you'll see people there,
Some will sit in their "need some love chair."

There are many, like the sands at the shore,
Like you, looking for love, and nothing more.

So, open your heart if you really dare,
And find yourself one whose life you can share.

Mike Lemp

Love Potion

In love potion number one,
It makes your life with her so fun.
In love potion number two,
It insures your love for her is true.
In love potion number three,
It guarantees she will love just me.
In love potion number four,
Our love will last forevermore.
In love potion number five
It enables our love to thrive.
In love potion number six,
Love will be pure, there'll be no tricks.
In love potion number seven,
Our love will seem to come from heaven.
In love potion number eight
It makes our life and love so great.
The first eight are mixed together to make love po-
tion number nine,
And whenever you take it
your love will be divine.

Robin Dawn Hudechek

Tea Ceremony

I pour fragrant tea
press the cup into your hands
Our fingers touch.

Linda Singer

Then There Was

I let go of talking to myself,
experience the no-time of now,
just now, looking at the way
tiny hairs curl at your neckline,
at the way your nose widens at the tip,
at the calcium river carved on your thumbnail,
as it pinches my thigh.

This is the opposite of ego,
feeling the rapture,
worshiping the miracle,
there is only you,
you, no longer the other.

Daniel McGinn

Man With a Walker

Sits at a fast food diner, says a prayer,
unwraps his burger and forgets to eat.

Stares at the framed photo he's placed on the table,
stares at her for a while, burger in hand.

He listens to her like he used to listen to the radio.
She can make him laugh. She can make him cry.

He doesn't feel like eating but she tells him he has to.
She never liked this place

but she goes where he goes, waits patiently
in a photograph, smiling at him while he eats.

William S. Friday

"Stumbled"

I have stumbled
again and again
in my life
But I never landed
on my feet
until I stumbled
over you

Glen Nesbitt

Forever

Every second I'm at your beck and call.
Every minute I want you in it.
Every hour should be ours.
Every day with you I want to stay.

Every week you I seek.
Every month you I want.
Every season your love is pleasin'.
Every year I want you near.

Every decade we've got made.
Every generation, a celebration.
Every century you're all I need.
Every millennium want you for every one.

Every era I want you there-a.
Until eternity, I'll love you certainly.
Until infinity, we'll have unity.
When you think we're done,
Infinity plus one.

Anthony Fitzgerald

Century

This day was foretold the moment I was born.
I had looked forward to it.
I had rehearsed it ninety-nine times.

The first twenty were of growing,
The next thirty were unchanging,
And the last forty-nine were of decline.

I have grown old with the world.
The world has changed.
So have I.

But the world adapts to change,
Though I am crushed by it.
Is the pain worth being one hundred?

Thea Iberall

My Star Light

At 101, my mother stands on the fitness platform
trying to make a virtual hoola-hoop go round
and round. She swings her hips left and right
but the character on the screen doesn't move.
The pressure of her feet and knees and rocking
hips are weightless, without force as if she isn't
here, as if she's already as light as stardust or
unbound like photons traveling for
three thousand years

Jeri Thompson

Working Out

Women in yoga pants, wearing blue eye shadow
and red nail polish, prance in for aerobics.
I go in wearing sweats, towel, headphones
and head for the lifecycle.
What I want to know is this –
why is sweat dripping off my chin and nose
while they get dates with men who drive Porsches?

Michael Cantin

A Weight Loss Poem, -Or- Myself, Abridged

My pants no longer fit,

I discover.

For as I climb the stairs

they descend.

Jerry Garcia

Elevators

This
is all I want
to say
about
elevators:

Get me off
at the
next floor

if your
only intent
is to look
at me

with conviction
and rage
some desire
and a lot
of red lipstick.

MJ

"A Simple Smile"

You don't need a sense of piety
to understand ubiety
Just give yourself a chance
to feel
the space you're taking up

It isn't all about the way you feel
or what you think
might be congruent
Communication
isn't only
languages in which we're fluent

Everyone can tell you about a time
that they said everything
with just
a simple smile
They knew words
would
never
do

When vernacular is lacking
Let your volume speak for you

Aseah Sabir

Pink and White Pillow

A bouncy castle bridge.
"P" for a perfect, soft dream
a cozy silver eye hole
a fluffy thunderbolt of sleepiness
Pink white and blue rainbow
full of good ideas.
A curved arrow
Sweet sleepy airplane.
Fuzzy snowflakes
Water fountains wet wish
Smooth face
Magical soft fluff
Squishy magnifying glass
Puffy fluffy cakes full of hot chocolate

Time to sleep people,
Please!

Lydia Quevedo

Nocturn

Night lends a most solitary sentiment;
not lonely, or sad,
but peaceful.
You and your thoughts
and the moon, the night,
and dew, are a
single
entity. There's a sense of a greater,
a sense of companionship;
not God, a single presence, yet simultaneously
expansive and intimate.
Thoughts condense
like dew on grass, and stress fades
like the heat of the day;
peace and calm joy
rise
like mist in moonlight,
and under the populous sky splattered
with flecks of stars,
shards of moon,
you are alone
and the world turns calm around you.

Cassidy Kao

The Zodiac Family

Libra is coming
Scales, light, ready for justice
The pair of true scales

Then we see Cancer
A crab, curious, naughty
A quite measly crab

Then, Virgo swirls by,
Beautiful, distressed, tired
A searching goddess

Jennifer Bradpiece

Illumination

Star bent burglar,
pull the curtain back.
Rain the glitter
down towards my
open palms.

Some will settle
under my pinky nail.
Some will swirl
the eyelash night closed.

What is left
we will stack
dutifully like bricks,
amassing starlight
until each sleeping creature
is visible
and glowing.

Cindy Rinne

Spirals
After "Lights Labyrinth" by Ludmila Pawlowska

Cut spiral

Infinite space
Matches symbol

On my bracelet
Eternal movement

Ripples wet
Central carve

Negative space

Oil on water
People and

Divine

Jasper
Moonstone holds

Wrist spiral eye
In palm

Hamsa protects

Natalie Yee

Waves

Life is like a wave
with thousands of
smaller waves
constantly coming and going
in no pattern

Each pit, an obstacle
Then an increasing slope
To a peak, an accomplishment
So many different heights
So many different kinds

Multiple waves
Pass through at the same time
A big test, a piano competition,
A good grade on a project
Ups and downs simultaneously

Even in the lowest times
The wave will climb back up
Never forget that
The bad times
Will pass

Marisa SK Gasper

Does It Matter?
4/15/15

Though neurons fire
In material reality,

The end result
Has no

Mass.

Clifton Snider

The Now, or Nothing at All

Only scientists
could name a galaxy
EGS-zs8-1
13.1 billion light-years from us,
born 675 million years after
the Big Bang
(current creation myth).

Three telescopes
assembled the picture:
a blue-white splotch
surrounded by a darker blue aura,
then total black.

Further than any other galaxy
yet discovered,
it may, in this present moment,
be dead,
dissolved to invisible matter,
or nothing,
nothing at all.

Clifton Snider

No Worries

Phobos--Greek god of fear,
son of Mars & Aphrodite--
circles Mars with his brother,
Deimos (god of terror).

Phobos circles Mars
every 7 hours and 39 minutes,
so close, scientists say,
it will burst into fragments
and become a ring around
the planet, flinging rocks
into its surface
in 20 million years
        or so.

William S. Friday

"Planet Oklahoma"

I grew up on a moon
orbiting
the planet Oklahoma

David Ohlsen

I Wanna Be a Space Detective

Because who wouldn't?

I don't know what I would do
exactly
but I know that I would wear
a really cool hat.

The hat would have lasers
and could project alien disguises
onto my ruggedly handsome face.

I'd buzz around star systems
rescuing rich, blue skinned dames
from their cold and calculating lovers,
laughing as I made the jump to lightspeed
with half the galaxy on my tail
and bars of gold pressed latinum
jingling in my coat pocket.

I'd bring swagger and retribution
to lonely planets
who have forgotten
how to smirk.

HanaLena Fennel

Gelid as a Looking Glass

A lattice
Extending in all directions
Exhaling itself into solid

Sapphire
Gypsum

Frost flower finger tips
Purpose them as a bite and hold

Greek, both for "ice" and "rock"

Snowflake
Diamond

Arms aslant, gamble at defense
Burden your body to counter supplication of your
eyes

Obsidian
Silk, as a liquid

Each surface cut to disperse
This is the angle of your chin, the cut of your hip
The distance of your beauty

Y.K. Watts

Reflection

throw me your stones
I will stand
still
shield myself with
love
underneath the burning sun.

with open arms
I welcome you
with tear-stained feet
planted in
blood-stained dirt.

this body you break
is a mirror of your
hate
painfully projecting your own
reflection.

Rebekah Yospe

Vampires

They have pale skin

Teeth as sharp as a murder knife

A cape as smooth as silk

When they pierce your neck you won't know

All of the sudden blood is gushing from your neck

No one is there you're about to pass out but you can't

Your world is upside down

Your skin is becoming pale

And suddenly you're craving blood

You can't get the nearest person

Health reasons......

And now you noticed you're not in the mood for junk food

That garlic bread for dinner makes you sick and you can't read

That family you have doesn't exist

All of your pets scared of you and you smell like death

Nathan Estrick

Knight Rupert Always Comes At Night

The night of Christmas Eve
Knight Rupert always comes at night
In a sleigh drawn by dragons,
The front one sickly green.
Knight Rupert always comes at night
His helmeted face fell
Knight Rupert always comes at night
With dark chains to drag bad children,
screaming into hell.

Knight Rupert always comes at night
There's nothing you can do;
Knight Rupert always comes at night
Your evil acts, through his evil
You will always rue

Crystal Dawn Hayes

I Am Hate

I am hate and all that it means,
I am the horror in all of your dreams,
I am the torment that lurks in your past,
I am the one that you think of last,
I am the evil in all that you do,
and if you hate me,
it's because I am you.

Mean Girls

They can be manipulating, sneaky, and snotty.
Mean girls are all kinds of naughty.
Giving you dirty looks behind your back,
Those girls always have something they lack.
Using you and hating you.
Jealous of you and befriending you.
They will do anything to make you feel insecure too.
Mean girls double-cross.
They always think they are the boss.
They're too obsessed texting, vanity, and slang.
I'm so done with this game!
12-inch heels and short inappropriate dresses,
They make lasting emotional messes.
Flirting with guys.
There's always time for fun!
They make other girls want to run.
TV, and movies, shopping and boys.
They're midnight parties make so much noise.
Too talkative and say "totes" all the time.
Mean girls are sourer than a lime.
Bikinis and bras, lipstick and blush.
They are always in a rush.
Mean girls are annoying and they will never stop
coming.
Personally, I would have a better time fixing the
plumbing.

Sarah ChristianScher

Haunted House

no ghosts in the closet
no ghosts under the bed
no ghosts in the mirror
no ghosts under the sheets
no ghosts in the cupboard
but don't look up
don't look up
don't look up
she's on the ceiling
and she hates being stared at

Trista Hurley-Waxali

Real Things

Ghosts,

      little dogs
      and hungry middle school kids with guns

If none of these terrify you, then
      you're an Angelino.

Lilith Lanier

The Trouble With Sisters

The trouble with sisters
is they never leave you alone.
The trouble with never being left alone
is you never get peace and quiet.
The trouble with never getting peace and quiet
is you never get to think.
The trouble with not thinking
is you never get to learn anything.
The trouble with not learning
is you don't know anything.
The trouble with not knowing anything
is your brain begins to atrophy.
The trouble with brain atrophy
is you turn in to an Australopithecine.
The trouble with becoming an Australopithecine is you
would have to live 5 million years ago.
The trouble with living 5 million years ago
is you wouldn't have modern technology.
The trouble with not having modern technology is you
wouldn't be able to play Candy Crush!
The trouble with not playing Candy Crush,
is you wouldn't have anything to do when you're bored.
The trouble with not having anything to do when you're
bored is you would have to play with your sister...and
you already know the trouble with sisters!

Robert Lanphar

St. Denis Corridor of Lights

What a beautiful invitation
A simple stroll along
My church corridor of lights
With my breath prayer
Calling for connection
Receiving confirmation.

Lynne Bronstein

Prayer For The Little Girl In The Wheelchair

Is there no one
To take care of us all
The eternally sad
The preternaturally hungry
The perpetually in the dark
The always cold
The insatiably dreaming
The disappointed in lust
The questioning in love
The tired in belief
The restless in singing
The crying in celebration
The lonely in a house
The traveler in the city
The grace of us all.

Moira Ward

Thinking

Thinking, thinking, delving deep,
Into the memories that sleep.
They leave me breathless,
Quiet and restless.
Thinking, thinking, forevermore,
Memories open that sacred door,
Freeing my eyes to cry their tears,
Thinking, thinking through the years.
Memories old and once forgotten,
Break the surface, moldy and rotten.
Thinking, thinking, never-ending,
Of the wounds these tears are mending.
Thinking, thinking, of the end,
How it may be just 'round the bend.
Thinking, thinking of my breath,
And how it will stop after death.

Alannah Jordan

Be You

No sunset is the same
Just as no one is the same
We express ourselves
Through different shades
Of purples and oranges and reds
Different clouds
Poufy clouds and soft strokes across the sky
Stars in the sky shining with all their might
Having that single space in the universe
Specifically for them and them alone
We are sunsets and stars
We are the sky and the clouds
We are the sun and the moon
We are in Nature
Nature is in us
Everything you do, say, and think is ok
Everything you see, feel, and want is ok
Everything you hate, can't stand, and angers you is ok
Everything you don't like, will never like, and might
start to like is ok
Everything you think is amazing, irresistible, and
incredible is ok
Everything is ok

Kelsey Bryan-Zwick

Dear Girls,

Dear girls, hold your heads up high
when they tell you (and they will)
that such-and-such is not for girls
or that boys are just better at it
whatever it may be, it is worth chasing

Do not be afraid to look the scoundrels
in the eyes, to voice clearly, "Then I
shall be the first," and please know
that with my whole heart, I believe you
always have, and always will

With love
yours truly

Lori McGinn

I Am Not This Person Lost In The Family Tree

Sitting on a branch, contemplating Sylvia Plath
It is a jungle up here
I am making friends with the snakes
I am English
blue veined china
I break easily
I am Oakie
dry mouthed, dusty
backwoods and barefoot, with
blueberry hands, wildflower hair
I am Cherokee
when I dream, I speak their language
I wear my skin like the plague
dead
dry
falling
I am Irish
my heart is green
my spirit, Celtic
I am Jewish by adoption
I cry
Abba Father
Pray
for the peace of Jerusalem

Raquel Reyes-Lopez

If No Saint Appears

In the crack of the egg, olive oil stir,
and the sizzle in frying there's a symphony
composing itself. Add a touch of basil
when it's almost at the end of its song.

Heat up tortillas. Let them burn a little
because the face of La Virgen de Guadalupe,
or Jesus might appear on them. It depends
on how worrisome the prayer is.

If the following morning
no saint appears on your toast,
it only means nothing has died.
Pound at your heart if you must,
as long as you need to, but love
still lives.

Megan Richtman

Field of Gravestones

Lights splashed off the drizzly pavement
We walked, hand in hand, laughing at snowflakes in
our hair
These memories of you pressed in my mind like
daphnes
Between the letters we wrote when you were far away

And I won't say I'm in love as much as I would like to
And you, you hate goodbyes, so instead I'll say I—
I forget you.

Lily Krol

Watching, Wondering, Waiting, Why? *

When will my Father come back?
He probably won't come back from war.
Blood red as velvet. Think good thoughts.

He still wondered and waited.
He won't come back, what a terrible, horrible thought.
Years waiting for his Father to come back
in the dark empty small room.

Only a few more days, what a good thought, but his
Father never came back.
Droop drip drop went his tears.
Droop drip drop went his Father's blood.
Tears filled his eyes.
Blood covered the swords. Bloody armor with dead
bodies in them.
The tears filled the funeral.
Embarrassed
Of his tears.
Silently. Crying in a small corner
Of the small, dark,
Empty room.

* Poem based on Rembrandt's
Boy In The Red Vest

Carter Moon

The Signal Is Dying

The radio tower
Whips in the squall,
As backs bend
To escape the wind.

Only nicotine and God
Will keep our hands
Churning now.

The signal is dying,
But there was
Probably no one
Listening anyhow.

I am tired
And you are a husk.
At least the dirt is soft
And the sun is dead.

Photosynthesis will
Sprout seeds stuck in skulls
Come morning.

You and I,
Of the same earth,
Blessed at least to live
In last gasps
Than die in the gas.

Lotus Cloud

Because We Are Frightened

Because we are frightened
remember we're scared
Our children have never
felt sun or fresh air

We all have been hiding
deep under the earth
We old ones remember
the wind and our mirth

Our children are restless
the elders are dying
Peddlers have stopped coming
for we have stopped buying

Perhaps the men left
could we run free
Yet if they are gone
then where would we be

Does our forest remain
do the flowers still bloom
Have the men gone away
or left us with doom

Erin Milne

Hope

My hope is a golden fire, brighter than the sun.
Hope is a dandelion, strong and proud.
Hope will not fall to storm, nor rain,
Nor to heavy tread.
Hope will always fall,
Just to spring back up again
And ask
Did you miss me?

Emma Morrison

Walking

I walk past trees and bushes
Past creatures hiding in logs and under stones
In front of me is a farm
My farm
Well, my family's farm
I walk closer and closer until I see my horse's pasture
Home I am, at last

Marc Cid

River Rover

The river at my window
woke me with
enthusiastic bubbling
flowing free
and rippling, lapping
tail-wagging joy
The heavy rains
bringing it to the city
for the first time this season
The river rolls over
begging to be petted

Robbi Nester

Seal

Clearly these mammals have imagination.
I watched one spin in place,
eyes closed, as I did once at 5,
falling in a dizzy heap to watch
the room spin, the familiar
turning alien but quickly taking shape
again within accustomed walls.
The seal though kept its eyes
shut tight, a meditative whirling
like a sufi's dance. His eyelids
never quivered as he spun,
bobbing a bit in the enclosure,
calm face composed,
resembling a dead pharaoh
wrapped tight within his gold
sarcophagus, entering the realms
of the next world, dreaming
a life relentless as the tides.

Sophia Larsen

Horses

A gentle eye,
A strong, chestnut neck,
A steady, powerful set of legs,
A broad, strong back.
Strong enough to serve a master,
Gentle enough to carry children,
But always ready to run and graze in a meadow
and frolick in the shade.
Horses are noble creatures,
Strong, steady and brave.

Taylor Joneleit

Deep in The Heart of Africa

Deep in the heart of Africa,
Five friends defend their home.
Listen close and I'll tell you their names,
And of the terrain they still roam.
Fuli, the fastest, a cheetah with speed,
Ono, an egret with the keenest of sight,
Bunga, a honey badger who's done
the bravest of deeds,
Beshte, the hippo who's the strongest,
both day and night,
And the leader of this gang, the fiercest by far,
A lion cub named Kion,
with a Roar heard from afar,
Now what they always say,
Before taking off to help one astray:
Till the Prideland's end,
Lion Guard defend!

Maggie Magana

There Once Was A Cat Named Pat

There once was a cat named Pat
who always slept in a hat
he jumps on the bed
and sits on his head
and always tore up the mat.

Aseah Sabir

I am a Wonderful Creature

I am a feather from a phoenix.
I am a blue cotton candy horse.
I am a fish swimming in Laffy Taffy.
I am a rainbow ice-cream meadow.
I am a blue glitter arctic fox playing in blueberry snow.
I am a shiny purple eagle swinging in the clouds.
I am a flaming fire red color.
I am a shimmer lake on the moon.
I am 1,000's of crystals of snowflakes shining in the sun.
I am the winter breeze.

Graham Smith

four valentines

may love
bring you hope
in your spring

may love
bring you joy
in your summer

may love
bring you wisdom
in your fall

may love
bring you warmth
in your winter

Robert Lanphar

Redondo Beach in Shroud

The lifeguard station, closed
The volleyball courts, dormant
The beach sands, void
The activity trails, sparse
The fog rolling in to an expectant mournful horn
The lights bathed in mists
The surf breaking in a plaintive pace
The sun reduced to a glow
The flags in flaccid attention

How my spirits soar in kind
As I join with my environment

Mari Maxwell

Winter Étude

In the Connemara rains
soft, sighing mists embrace lichen,
bog and boreen.
At dusk, the dried ferns breathe fire.
Gnarled blackberry husks
hum in fading light.

Across the boreens hay-humped farmers
pedal rusted bikes through raw wind and
puddled laneways.
To where –
they whisper affection
to their lumbering charges.

A new moon slides in.
Inky, cold, dollops of hail,
frying our windows
'tween winter and spring.

In the shed the kittens gather;
clods of turf their winter bed.
Lethargic bundles entwined –
feral and domestic.
Peaceful in the gathering gales.
Dark and light. Tame and wild.
Pause to the watcher.

Lori McGinn

Winter Comes Knocking On My Back Door

her eyes are a vortex of sorrow
rosebud mouth forming questions

hanging from her frail shell of a body
is her favorite blue wool coat
pockets stuffed full of post-it notes to God

She opens her mouth
breathes out a cloud of roses
into the living room sky

Laying under her rosy ceiling
she curls up, hand in God's
with a sweet surrender, offers her last smile.

Stephen Howarth

Soundless Song

Soundless she sleeps: her breathing so slight,
She could be a doll, or dead.
Curled up, quiet, a little movement of dream
Steals across her – quiver of a moment,
Shiver, and calm. With a tiny sigh she turns,
Lies still again, and in this silent sleeping
Dreams silent dreams. Pictures lighten
Her night and day, pictures of creatures,
Trees, grass, people, moving and mouthing,
And soundless as her sleeping, every one.
Neither a doll, nor dead; just deaf.
I reach down, touch her, whisper her name.
Unhearing, she wakes, turns to my smile,
And in silence, our eyes speak of love.

Annie Neal

My Favorite Fairytale Is

My favorite fairytale is
when Cinderella climbed the beanstalk,
and Jack went to the ball.
Wait- that's not it!

My favorite fairytale is
when Little Red Riding Hood met a giant,
and three goats went to their grandmother's house.
Wait- that's not it!

My favorite fairytale is
when Snow White was huffing and puffing,
and the bad wolf met seven dwarves.
Wait- no, no, no!

My favorite fairytale is
when a girl named Annie wrote a story about,
her favorite fairytale.
Yes, that was the one!

Lotus Cloud

I Am A Fairy

I am a fairy
I live in the flowers
I do my good deeds
(which I practice for hours)

My hair is all golden
My eyes are like stars
My diet is of honey
and chocolate bars

One day I was playing
alone in the woods
I spied an old woman
displaying fine goods

So I bought a silk scarf
and a pair of blue shoes
and I danced with my friends
till a quarter of two

But then the men came
and chased us away
and we are too frightened
to come out and play

Terry McCarty

Red Wind

the red wind blows hard,
and when rain comes,
the drops sting like cactus needles
so I run for shelter
under what's left of a house
and the ceiling falls
on top of my head
so I run from shelter

I see people walking around
as if everything's normal,
they claim there's no wind--
and I'm just having a daydream

maybe they're right
but I still see the Crimson Twister
tearing apart Main Street
like Godzilla risen from the ocean
and my aunt's house
has a backyard storm shelter
over on Elm--
two blocks away--
wish me luck

Briannah Milne

Bravery

Bravery is no blanket,
It does not hide you from fear,
Nor does it shield you from its icy breath.

Bravery is no sword,
It does not cut down fear,
Nor does it sever its spikey thorns.

Bravery is no butterfly,
It does not spread like wildfire,
Nor does it spark from within.

Bravery is not the absence of fear,
Nor is it letting fear consume you,
Without fear there is no bravery.

Bravery is being scared,
Staring fear in the eye,
And then moving on.

Scarecrow

I made myself a scarecrow
as scary it could be
I thought
I'd keep it as
a friend to let it stay with me
I made the scarecrow
a bed and some blankets too,
and every time in the morning
I forget it's there and
I always get scared of
It.

Ellen Webre

Headdress

My sisters have often claimed
that in their prime (about ten years ago)
they had been glorious to look upon,
glowing with arms around their waists
and fingers in their hair.

But I, with a sinewy figure,
and hair blacker than my pupils
need not be tactlessly adorned
with dismembered limbs-
A cluster of white spiders will suffice

John Alvarado

A Spider on the Ceiling

A spider on the wall is not a threat at all.
A spider on the floor? A nuisance, nothing more.
But I get a creepy feeling from a spider on the ceiling.

I fear it just might dare
Drop stealthily into my hair,
Laying eggs while it's there.

One-thousand spiderlings would hatch one day!
Down my head crawling, they'd make their way,
To disappear without a trace
Into the orifices of my face.

Oh, such horror I cannot abide,
So, I step over to one side,
And upon that spider clinging high
Keep ever a watchful, wary eye.

Neela Michelsen

Room of Curly Singers

In the room of curly things, everything sung. Some of the singing is great, like lollipops, their sweet melody drifting across the room. But, the French Fries' singing was so bad it made your ears pop even though you are not traveling up a mountain. The beans from the Chicka tree rattle while they sing. The person who thinks you're crazy says, "cuckoo!" over and over as the trees swing back and forth, dancing. The tires rolled around the trees and the spring sang opera so loud that the glass shattered. The fireworks blasted everywhere singing their high-pitched tune as the wigs bopped their bouncy hair to the music. And Saturn's rings spun around the room making soft and loud sounds as you realize that you are singing too.

Alan Passman

On Bemoaning

The listless wind whines,
I'm just a man
whose shadow casts as much
as a dandelion.

If you blow me a kiss
then my head will come apart
just the same.

With that breath there
is no standing still,
just dancing in place.

Wonder if you see me.
Not necessarily
like I see you,
but at all.

Seth Halbeisen

Boredom in a Training Room

When I want to see the world shake,
I eat a pretzel.
If it is particularly hard,
I can see the movement in the air.
It's safe to say I like pretzels,
though I don't really know how
eating them can be so
world shakingly effective.
I love to see the images
in the monitors shake,
like there is an earthquake
that only I can see.
Like an act of God is
happening within my mouth,
and it is glorious.
God I need another pretzel.

Briannah Milne

Pineapple

Alas, my love's eyes have grown dull.
What were once green flames erupting from her head,
Are now withered and grey eels.
Her beautiful spikes are no longer,
Replaced by brown wrinkles.

I can no longer hear,
The breeze rustle her hair.
What was once a beautiful scent,
Has now turned sickly sweet.
Age has not been her friend.

Though I shall never hear her voice,
Nor know the sight of her smile.
Her skin more like scales,
She knows I will always love her.
My dear, sweet pineapple.

Paige Kunkle

Dear Cut Up Pineapple,

I am so sorry. I had no idea they would cut you up after you were ready. They cut you up without thinking twice. I could never cut you up like that. You had a great life. We went in the beach. We went in the water. You looked amazing with the pearly water splashing against your green leaves. It all came to an end on that sad day. I had gone to school. When I got back they were eating you. I was depressed. But, I have to admit you were pretty good.

Carlisle Huntington

Ode to Black Coffee

I remember the day,
When I acquired the taste for black coffee.
 Bitterness awoke me,
a thousand tiny needles
stabbing my tongue.

I remember the day,
Before I could keep it down.
Cup clouded with cream,
until that rich blackness
was an agreeable creamy beige,
warm, sweet, soft.
That was what the world was like,
Back then,
flowing with milk and honey,
Now I am awake.

Some wonder how I keep it down;
some would rather sleep walk,
than stomach the taste.
I tell them the truth,
it never tastes like you think.

Josiah Knox

Cold Sparkling Water

It looks like snowflakes
floating up from a glassy pool.
It smells like nothing,
but when it goes into your nose,
it tickles.
Soft bubbles
popping on your finger tips
as your hand is surrounded
by cool water.
It feels relaxed
like you are floating
in the middle of a vast ocean
with only bubbles popping in your ears.
The sound of tiny roly-polies
being dropped from above
in the dark.
fizzy little water bubbles
popping in your mouth.

Kaleb Moniz

Pizza

Pizza is good
I'd eat a ton if I could
Oodles and oodles of cheese
give me some please

Tomato sauce is tasty
when I see it, I get hasty
Crunchy crunchy crust
no need to adjust

Delightful and delicious
oh, how it is nutritious
Pizza is yummy
and will always be savored in my tummy

Ayaan Sheik

Cotton Candy

It's a puffy pillow.
A big letter "Y" for yummy
Makes me say "mmmmmmm"
A lightening bolt of candy
A rainbow in a cloud Coo-Coo Land
An airplane that left a trail of sugar.
Sweet snowflakes of strawberry, blueberry bubblegum
flavor.
A fountain making candy water
And everyone drinks it with happiness.
Mystical saliva makes everything disappear.
Cotton Candy.
And the world goes to sleep.

Cheese and Crackers, Crackers and Cheese

Cheese and crackers,
Crackers and cheese.
I could eat them forever.
Please? Please?
Might I have some cheddar and saltine?
Colby and wheat?
I'll eat ANY cheese, on ANY cracker!
Maybe add some peanut butter.
Every day, I am heard to utter.
Might we have more cheese and crackers?
Oh dear.
All gone, gone, Oh fear!
Emergency run to the market.
The dairy and snack aisles, are my targets
Gasp.
NO!
NO!
THEY'E ALL SOLD OUT!
I begin to pout.
I scream.
I cry.
I bought them all yesterday.

Micah Kunkle

Music, Film, Rhyme

It's all divine
Image barers,
were creative lairs,
but sin has cursed humankind
and has corrupted our minds
beauty, and brokenness
it's all a mess
Now you may think that this isn't true
but then my question is,
what's your worldview?

Marie Lecrivain

The Difference Between

What's real, and what's not doesn't matter
when the news hits close to home. Your poor heart
beats once - then falls to the floor to shatter
in a million little fragments that start
to spin in counter-clockwise anger
in response to the chaotic carnage
splashed across the TV screens. Now, beware
the conclusions that you'll draw, the garbage
churned out by media fascists who thrive
as the mote in your eye, and the base voice
that quietly convinces you to strive
for ignorance. This time, you have a choice;
you can salvage your soul or let it die.
Listen hard for the truth - or live the lie.

Natalie Yee

Without Knowing

The fear in their eyes
The helpless souls
The skinny bodies
The longing faces
The sagging tails
The dirt in their fur

Barely enough food
Just enough water
A small cage
Shared with many others
No bed to sleep
No space to move

No owner to love them
To pet them
To give tummy rubs
To care for them

An owner who wants money
Who only cares about money
Who doesn't care a bit about the dogs
Who tortures innocent puppies
Who does all this for greed

But, people buy these puppies
Everyday, at pet stores
Without knowing

Ellie Sommer

At The Little Corner Pet Shop

At the little corner pet shop,
where you hear the cat's yowl.
At the little corner pet shop,
there are creatures on the prowl.
Shrieking, squeaking, growling, squawking
Yellow eyes gleam from thick cage bars.
Look.
Something in its mouth is wriggling about.
"Don't worry," said the Manager as he walked over,

"She's really sweet and doesn't bite.

Go on, pick her up. Hold her."

As your wheeled out on your stretcher,
thing still dangling from your thigh, you hear
"So sorry," from the Manager, and
"come back again, next time".

Victoria Irwin

Don't Let It Bite

The Monster underneath my bed
is closer than a pet,
He likes to bark and growl and scratch
but he won't eat me yet

The Closet Beast is nicer still
and often prone to clanging,
He likes to pull apart my tops
but keeps my sweaters hanging

I have had a cat, a dog, a bird
a hamster and a lizard,
But monsters are the only pets
that want to eat my liver

Lisa Ramirez

The Walking Dead

Pitch black   bloody red

Running   yelling   stopping

Prison   zombies   cars   food

Limping   bleeding   hiding

Rotten   scary

Peopleammo.

Bernardo Aragon

Zombie Sandwich

A zombie sandwich is easy to make
All you do is simply take
One slice of bread
One slice of human brain
Some blood
One ripped arm

One zombie
One piece of string
A dash of salt
That ought to do it
And now comes the problem…
Tell that zombie I am not food

Raundi K. Moore-Kondo

The Last Thing I Want to See Before I Die*

is the inside of the mouth
of something large enough
to devour me whole

It might decide to toy
with me first
and chase me
around the yard

Paw at my tail
as I try to run and hide

Sniff and nudge me
while I play dead

Trap me beneath
one giant paw
to gnaw on my tougher parts

Suck out every flavor
until I am a tender
tasteless bore

Then toss me into the air
and swallow me
alive.

For Brendan Constantine

Heather Noel Aldridge

Hair of the Cat

I'll take a double Blood, on the rocks
A slice of dissolved expectations
A few sprinklings of bitterness
Throw in a dash of lost hope
Add a twist of fate to taste
Shaken and stirred to a pulp
Pour over freshly plucked thorns
Garnish with a sigh
Serve with an assortment of mouth-watering Lies

Aaron Vega

Recipe for a Monkey Taco

A monkey taco is easy to make all you do is simply
take
1 piece of hair
1 stack of smashed avocado
Some bear meat
1 chicken leg
1 hard shell taco
1 monkey
1 banana
1 dash of salt
That has to do it
And now comes the problem
To tell the monkey to stop swinging

Marisa SK Gasper

Bar Boys Bore

Your "drinking personality"
Leaves much to be desired,
Like a personality.

When you go to the bar -
Or drink and can't shut up,
I am bored to tears.

How a drunken rant
Babbles and drools...

Insignificant, pointless chatter -
To hear yourself talk.

Jerry Garcia

Carolyn Sings Backup

In this arena of sight
and sound
the shadowed chorus
refrains harmony
on a fifty-foot stage.
Carolyn's intimate but broad
tonal palette resonates.
Black hair drapes
her spaghetti strap frame,
hips sway like fantails,
arms are dancing cobras.
Glossy wide lips sing me
into heaven.

Sweet-voiced and pretty,
she passions like a poet
in overbites of stage light
among air gulps
playing for attention.
This raven-haired chanteuse
forever whispers my heart to
                    sleep.

Robert Rodriguez

Visual Stimulation

We met
At the track
These eyes
And her booty
It was a thing of beauty
Captivating
Hypnotizing
And motivating
Walking turned to jogging
Breathing
Soon became heavy
Muscles tightened
Legs got weak
And yet
That booty
Kept tired legs
Pushing
Further
Further than they've gone in a while
Until
Shortness of breath ended the jog
Our moment
Gone
Her booty
Just what these lazy thighs needed
Hoping for another glance
Went around the track
A few more times

And
Just in case
This booty
Too
Motivated another

David Ohlsen

I Wanna Be A Judge

Because if I was a judge
I'd get to wear silky robes all day
and sit in a high chair.

When I enter the courtroom
everyone would have to stand up
and call me 'honorable.'

My wooden gavel would be so big
I'd have to make
a super strong robotic arm
just to bang it.

I'd be good to the good people,
bad to the bad people,
and have the wisdom to know
that most people
are a bit
of both.

Thomas R. Thomas

this moment

this moment
between sleep
and wakefulness

I lie still
within my
imagination

enveloped
in the dream
not ready yet

to approach
so called
reality

Marc Cid

Bedhead

Today I'll stay
in bed and think
of all the people
I'll never meet
no matter how many
steps I take
whether by will
or hand of fate

And then I'll think
of those I've met
have yet to meet
forget regret

Ron Feldman

Spirit Guide

My beach has an allure for some,
a hint of what's beyond.
Most can't get past the waves,
though I try to be as gentle
and accommodating as I can.
And then there are the brave
and wonderful few
who explore my depths and experience me
at close to my full strength.

Vaughan Risher

My Shark

Every time
I see his face
It's either sneering or smirking

Maybe he's looking at me.

I imagine all the pent up jealousy and
bottled up frustration contributes

I heard she saw him yesterday

Doesn't know him

I don't know him
But if she gets to know him,
like the last girl did

I don't know if I'll be able to keep it all bottled
for much longer

A shark can be caught
And slipped into a transparent cage,
and the delicate flower can then grow
in the heady atmosphere
surrounding its aquatic prison

But the glass cracks,
Eventually

Candy Ayala

Beach

Large waves crash on sand
You can make a sandcastle
Blue water shimmers

Don Kingfisher Campbell

Always Been a Surfer

As a teen I loved
surfing the hills
of Monterey Park
on my bicycle

(I even played
a surfer boy
in a Garvey Junior High
English class production)

Later living
in San Gabriel
I surfed channels
looking for good movies

(My only try
at body surfing
in Huntington Beach
resulted in a dislocated knee)

Now in Alhambra
I surf the internet
on a laptop every day
to find inspiration for poems

(I love surfing
the lines I create
making images
and metaphors as I go)

David Ohlsen

I Wanna Be a Writer

Because if I was a writer
I could wander around all day
thinking about
the most important things
in the world–

the things that I love,
the things that changed me,
and the things that I'd like
to change.

I'd attach old metaphors to new feelings,
like saying that pride
can be just as beautiful, and as dangerous,
as a pack of lions,
their emerald eyes captivating
all who cross their path.

I'd speak my heart
until my voice gives out,
and then
I'd pick up a pencil.

Warren Allen

Confessions of a Numbers Man

Well...
now where was I ...?
You had a cup full of numbers...
or maybe it was words...
They were jumbled up together...
They made a lovely blur...
And I...
can't even tell...
The difference between them...
Is there any at all...?
Did you ever notice?...
they're very small...
It's hard to count them ...
when you're starting...
to...
fall...

Gerald Locklin

Long Shot Double-Sequel

American Sniper
Shoots
The Martian

Ben Trigg

The Fire Dodging Chemist Burns Popcorn

It's not intentional, exactly.
It's more that flames follow him everywhere.
He is a study in survival skills.
The chemistry to put the fire out.
The dodging because he's not a good chemist.
Truth be told, he wanted to be a dancer.
He wishes he'd followed that dream.
At least then he could avoid the flames with beauty.

Jacob Munoz

Death by Rhyme

Ms. Poet wrote a lot
But one day she thought
Why do I only rhyme?
Surely one day I know I'll die
And I know there is more to do
Than just rhyme.
So then she went
In her car with dents
To the liqour store owned by Kyle
And went to the poetry aisle
And found a very large pile
Of poems on paper
Which later turned into water vapor.

Annelise Cramm

Writer's Block

Stopped up.
Like a cork in a bottle.
The words will not come.
The ideas cease to flow.
Frustration drives me batty.
Wanting to scream.
But my voice is gone

Allan Passman

Scrawled On a Box in My Closet

We fumble towards profundity
us poets, us back alley clowns
smeared and besmirched
in a mask of our own obscurity.

The makeup is slack with sweat,
but the skull beneath has the depth
of density. Heavy are the heads
wearing invisible crowns

that when exposed crumble, fall,
and become the chip
on the shoulder
of the literary incognito
destined to be shunned passive.

Jaimes Palacio

My First Poem Of The Night

Some poets begin their sets with beautiful
lovely poems about tiny birds.

And the beautiful, lovely flight of birds
flying in beautiful lovely sights.

And flowers that resemble beautiful lovely birds
in beautiful lovely meadows of beautiful lovely.

And lovely beautiful songs of birds singing
lovely and beautiful in the flowers.

And the beautiful lovely way it makes a poet
feel about beauty, and loveliness and birds.

And oh! The beauty!
And oh! The lovely!
And oh! The birds!

Some poets begin like that.
I am going to begin
by saying...

Erin Milne

The Grass is Greener on the Other Side

The grass is greener on the other side
Called a little bird
And I, a simple stone, a rock, let out an anguished
sigh.
For I, no matter how hard I heaved
And tried, could not move, for my body had died long
Ago
A squirrel took pity on me and asked,
Soon he carried me on his back,
He heaved and pulled
Then soon he cried "look!"
And behold, the grass on the other
Side!
But wait,
How could this be?
This grass is plain,
They are the same!
The grass is greener on the other side.

Naomi Ke'aloha Williams

The Bird is Beautiful

The Bird is Brown.
like the ground, the
Sun is out, the
Sky is beautiful
The tree is green
It is hot, but there
is a cool wind.
I love the bird,
the ground, the
Sun, sky, trees,
Weather. All the things.
I love you.

Alannah Jordan

Grow Up

Trees have leaves
Growing out of their trunks
It doesn't look like the picture perfect tree
It still grew around those pesky leaves
It grew just like you
In, seemingly, a blink of an eye
You were a little sprout in need of support
Now you stand before me with strong roots
Branches sturdy and structure
Stable and secure
You are the strong tree I knew you would be
Love all your imperfections and drawbacks
They are what make you, you
They make you a better, more experienced you
They make you aware as to what to do
And what not to do
The tree I knew you would be
The strong, unbreakable tree

Don Kingfisher Campbell

You Make Me Feel

like a blue
butterfly

on a pink
flower

like a black
millipede

sliding into an
earthen hole

like a gray
fox

snatching a white
chicken

like a green
Godzilla

stomping on
the rainbow city

and afterwards

like water
on a sidewalk

evaporating
in the sun

like the wicked
warlock of the west

melting
because of Dorothy

so this is how

God felt
creating

infinite
universes

Robert Jay

My Muse

Shows up whenever
She wants and leaves
Whenever she wants

With no considerate calling
Or even text messaging
First to let me know

But always unexpectedly and
Usually when I'm drunk

Spontaneous
Irreverent
Strong-willed
Unconventional
Like so many women
I love

Ben Trigg

If You Ask A Poet To Do Math

Certain liberties will be taken.
Solutions will be less exact,
more what feels right than what is correct.
Two plus two is always a surprise of the lighting
and ruminations on the poet's last kiss.

Glen Nesbitt

10 Hot Teachers

Ten teachers hot! hot!
Nine minutes after-school
Eight change into bathing suits and
Seven jump into the pool
Six come back after dinner
Five jump in the dark
Four teachers scream ah ah ah ah
Three get bitten by a shark
Two of the strongest lifeguards you have met
Jump into the pool to catch the big shark with a net
One lifeguard gets as close as you can get
Zero lifeguard fingers left.

Matthew Matusiewicz

End of the Line

If this is the end of the line
      Why was I the one who had to find it?
Why were you so surprised?
      Why was I the one who crossed the finish line first
Even though you were the one who placed it?
Why was I the one to leave you in the dust
      When I loved you so?
Why did I love you so?
Why was I the one left in the dark?

I guess I'm not expecting answers.
I guess I just miss you.

Carter Moon

Electric Ruination

Electric ruination haunts the empty spaces between us.
We may dance and call each other lovers,
So long as we acknowledge the dead corners inside us.
We may be bodies moving,
But don't take shelter in true love eternal even a
moment.
Do not pretend to never see the dimness;
Kavorkian shines his light behind my pupils,
And finds a soul in the midst of passing.

Do me the favor of acknowledging my tattered soul for
what it is,
Quilt, blowing in a breeze,
Stitched together by false memory twine,
Trying to remember why it's here
At all.

Mike Lemp

What is it?

It is what it is!

Is it what it is?

What it is, it is!

Is it, is it?

What?

Ellyn Maybe

Someday Our Peace Will Come

one day poetry dropped from the sky
and the animals grew iambic pentameter tails
and the people breathed in stars

one day music dropped from the sky
and the architecture turned symphonic
and the people breathed in harmony

one day memory dropped from the sky
and the past present and future sifted like flour
and the people breathed in wonder

smoke and ash
as distant as two sides of the same coin

A special thank you to Michael Y. Kondo,
Savanah R. Kondo, Graham Smith, Maggie Brown,
G. Murray Thomas, Ben Trigg, Steve Ramirez, JL Martindale,
Phil at The Ugly Mug, Paul and Hassan at It's A Grind.

Meet the Poets:

Heather Noel Aldridge: I work for the TV show "Criminal Minds," for 11 seasons, as a writer's assistant. I've been in love with poetry since I was a dorky, honors band-o in 6th grade, that desperately needed an outlet to express the churning emotions whirling within. Poetry has been the ultimate catharsis and I am forever indebted to this craft. Long live 6th grade awkwardness!
Plastered in Paris, 41
Hair of the Cat, 169

Warren Allen: I play music (guitar, etc.), as much as possible, essentially for the sound of it... but I find the lure of language irresistible too. I find all such things to be a fine starting point for friendships.
Waiting in Line, 69
Scraps, 75
Confessions of a Numbers Man, 183

John Alvarado mostly writes video-game software and lengthy Facebook posts. He occasionally enjoys wrestling with a poem and wonders why he doesn't indulge more often. He then fondly itemizes his wife, three kids, four cats, old home, full-time job, and running addiction.
A Spider on the Ceiling, 150

Bernardo Aragon likes to play soccer and write poems. His teacher is named Ms. Tatro; she teaches him about Poetry.
Zombie Sandwich, 167

Candy Ayala just published 3 poems in The Quest for Puma Poetry and loves sports.
Beach, 180

Vanessa Barrera is a soon to be sixth grader that loves dogs, blue, thrill rides, the beach, & is a multi-published poet.
Rollercoaster, 68

Sheri Black-Flynn: I'm a fifty-something + grammie of 10. I've been writing ever since I can remember although these days I have no time. I am not great, but I enjoy putting words together that in the end make sense.
Wine Stain, 54

Ruth Blue: I'm 16 and have been writing for many years. I've loved creating things and writing things for as long as I can remember. I'm one of the few who likes to write haiku.
Tadpoles, 8
Thunder, 22

Jennifer Bradpiece: I was born and raised in the multifaceted muse, Los Angeles, where I still reside. When I'm not rescuing Pit Bulls, I try to remain active in the Los Angeles writing and art scene, often collaborating with multi-media artists on projects. My poetry has been published in various journals, anthologies, and online zines, including Mad Poets Review, 491 Magazine, The Mas Tequila Review, & Redactions.
Changing Perception Is Possible, 60
Afternoon, 81
Illumination, 103

Lynne Bronstein has four books, four cats, and two Pushcart Nominations.
Prayer For The Little Girl In The Wheelchair, 121

Kelsey Bryan-Zwick dreams big (writes and draws) in Long Beach, California. She is a graduate of UCSC, with a B.A. in Literature/Creative Writing-Poetry. Kelsey's newest chapbook, Watermarked (Sadie Girl Press), intermixes poetry and artwork in bold tones.
Pebble and Tide, 4
Midwest Summer Bluegrass, 19
Dear Girls, 124

Briceida Campana is a 5th grader who loves having fun she is a intelligent student that never gives up!
BFF, 59

Don Kingfisher Campbell is publisher of the San Gabriel Valley Poetry Quarterly, host of Saturday Afternoon Poetry in Pasadena, California. For awards, features, and publication credits please go to: http://dkc1031.blogspot.com
Always Been a Surfer, 181
You Make Me Feel, 193

Michael Cantin is an aspiring poet and sloth fanatic residing somewhere in the wilds of Orange, California. He writes fitfully between bouts of madness and periods of lucid concern. You can find his work in The East Jasmine Review, Hobo Pancakes, several anthologies, and elsewhere.
First Step, 2
A Weight Loss Poem, -Or- Myself, Abridged, 97

Sarah ChristianScher is a poet trapped in a scientist's body. She lives in Pomona in a state of marital bliss with her husband, Ian. Sarah has been previously published in Silver Birch Press and the Lucid Moose Lit anthology, Like a Girl: Perspectives on Feminine Identity.
The Year the Sound Came From the Bottom of the Pacific, 16
Haunted House, 117

Marc Cid is a twenty-something living in Downey, California. Back in his day, there were only 150 Pokemon, and that was good enough for his generation. He's managed to go several years without running face-first into a glass door, but it's only a matter of time before their high command sends an elite squad of Windex'd Commandos after him again.
River Rover, 133
Bedhead, 177

Lotus Cloud is formally trained as a software engineer so she could make a living; she has been writing for pleasure as long as she can remember. This is her first public submission, including some of her earliest works.
Because We Are Frightened, 130
I Am a Fairy, 145

Annelise Cramm
Cheese and Crackers, Crackers and Cheese, 160
Writer's Block, 187

Amber Douglas is a poet, adventurer and snack food connoisseur who resides in Huntington Beach. She can be found reading her works at local SoCal venues.
Placebo Effect, 80

Nathan Estrick is a Californian, though he would not mind being in Middle Earth. He loves to read and write, and loves playing board games (especially the long ones). His favorite genre is fantasy, though sci-fi and superhero is great.
Knight Rupert Always Comes At Night, 114

Sara Faunce
Mean Girls, 116

Ron Feldman likes to blend technology, empathy, and creativity in his occupation as a software quality engineer.
Spirit Guide, 178

HanaLena Fennel was born on a goat farm in Oregon. From there, things got a little weird.
The Blue Truck, Twisted House, 67
Gelid as a Looking Glass, 111

Anthony Fitzgerald
What You Were and What I Am, 76
Century, 94

Rachel Foster is a writer from Southern California. She loves to watch reruns, sing while cooking and creating poems, often about food.
chores, 57

William S. Friday: Fictionary. 8 Megapixel Artist. Bloody Awful Poet. Bill Friday is a recently-published bender of Words, Voice, and Stuff. He can be heard on YouTube and read at bill-friday.com.
Stumbled, 92
Planet Oklahoma, 109

Jerry Garcia: A native of Los Angeles, poet, photographer and filmmaker. His poetry has appeared in a variety of anthologies and journals including: Askew, The Chiron Review, Palabra, Lummox Journal, Wide Awake: Poets of Los Angeles and Beyond and his chapbook Hitchhiking With the Guilty.
Elevators, 98
Carolyn Sings Backup, 172

John Gardiner teaches Shakespeare and Creative Writing at UCI. He writes poems and stories. He's been an actor, a poet, a radio host, a shape-shifter, and a human.
Coyote, 21
Loneliness, 83

Marisa SK Gasper is a writer, among other things...
She lives in a Los Angeles suburb with three to four cats.
Her grandparents wanted to be remembered as "helpful."
Does It Matter?, 106
Bar Boys Bore, 171

Bryan Gonzalez is a 5th grade boy who has poems in 2 books. Bryan also likes soccer, math & reading.
The Bicycle Ride, 63

Torrin A. Greathouse is a governing member of the Uncultivated Rabbits spoken word collective at UC Irvine and the 2015 winner of the Orange County Poetry Slam. Torrin's work has been published in several literary magazines and one chapbook, Cosmic Taxi Driver Blues. He is currently employed as the executive assistant of a sustainable lighting firm. His previous jobs include security guard, blogger, farm hand, antique store clerk and tattoo artist.
The Sky Fisher, 10
For The Ghost of Van Gogh's Ear, 33

Seth Halbeisen is male, human, and a resident of Earth (Third planet from the sun). He enjoys eating, making fun of himself, and other mildly active activities. Poetry is easier when sitting down.
Important Notes on Proper Table Manners, 53
Boredom in a Training Room, 153

Crystal Dawn Hayes: I have been writing poetry since childhood. My father also wrote but he wrote songs, I guess I inherited his talent. Most of my poems are on the darker side since I've had a lot of death and pain in my life. By channeling my feelings through writing I can cope with them easier.
I Am Hate, 115

Steven Hendrix has a B.A. in Comparative Literature and an M.A. in English Literature from California State University, Long Beach. His work has appeared in Chiron Review, Cadence Collective, Drunk Monkeys, Silver Birch Press, and Dead Snakes, among others. His favorite quote comes from his friend and mentor Ray Lacoste: "Be kind to each other; it's the last revolutionary act left."
Undertow, 7
Layers of Thirst and Dust, 18
Basquiat: Untitled (Life Study), 1983, 31

Darryl Henry has been published in the Quest Of Puma Poetry, he likes sports, and loves to play.
Go Carts, 64

Stephen Howarth is a professional author of history, a Fellow of the Royal Historical Society and of the Royal Geographical Society, a life member of the US Naval Institute, and a shy and tentative author of poetry. He has a Master's degree (with Distinction) in creative writing. Part English, part Scottish and half-Shetland by blood, he was born and brought up in England, and still lives there with a high cat quotient. He shares his heart between Shetland, Nottinghamshire and the USA.
Soundless Song, 143

Robin Dawn Hudechek as an MFA in poetry from UCI. Her poems have appeared in Caliban, Cadence Collective, Silver Birch Press, Poemeleon, Chiron Review and elsewhere. She lives in Laguna Beach, CA with her husband Manny and two beautiful cats.
Night Rose, 24
Tea Ceremony, 89

Carlisle Huntington is 18, from Dana Point California. Currently studying English at the University of Puget Sound in Tacoma Washington. Enjoys long walks and feminist rants.
Wild Heart, 14
On Shaving, 39
Ode to Black Coffee, 156

Trista Hurley-Waxali is a transplant from Toronto, now perched on barstools in West Hollywood. She has performed at Avenue 50, Stories Bookstore and internationally at O'bheal Poetry Series in Cork, Ireland and a TransLate Night show from Helsinki Poetry Connection. She is currently working on her novel, At This Juncture.
A Drawer Find, 42
Real Things, 118

Elizabeth Iannaci is a widely published Los Angeles-based poet, holds an MFA in Poetry, remembers when there really were orange groves, and shares birthdays with Red China and Julie Andrews.
Poems Written on Paper Made From Old Love Letters, 13
Fourth Floor Terrace, 40

Dr. Thea Iberall is called a "shimmering bridge between heart and mind." The Sanctuary of Artemis is a collection of contextual poems that explores the roots of Western patriarchal culture. Her visionary novel The Swallow and the Nightingale is about a 4,000 year old secret brought through time by the birds.
www.theaiberall.com
Separation, 11
My Star Light, 97

Canelle Irmas is a third year literature major and theatre minor in the UCSB College of Creative Studies. She is currently studying abroad in Scotland, working on scripts, and testing the waterproofing on her writer's notebook.
Water Spider, 20
There is Beauty in a Broken Watch, 36
The Setting Light, 48

Victoria Irwin lives with an army of cats (and one dog) outside of Austin, TX. She is the Editor in Chief of FangirlNation.com and gets out all of her weirdness writing for DirgeMag.com.
Don't Let It Bite, 165

Robert Jay lives in Long Beach where he also works as a longshoreman and occasionally writes when he's not busy waiting for lightning to strike.
My Muse, 195

Taylor Joneleit is 10 years old and lives in Anaheim. She gets some inspiration from her four and two year old brothers who run around her house tirelessly. She enjoys trying to catch lizards of all sizes, from inch long hatchlings to modern, ruler-sized dinosaurs.
Deep In The Heart of Africa, 136

Alannah Jordan is a junior in high school and her passion for writing has grown and will keep growing. She wants to have a career in either writing or music. She is very creative and loves to express herself through writing.
Be You, 123
Grow Up, 192

Cassidy Kao is 10 years old. She loves to write all kinds of poems. She has published two books, "Roller Coaster: a Kid's Guide on How to Write Poetry" and "Constellation Exploration: Greek Mythical Stories Retold with Simple Facts and Fun and Mysterious Riddles".
The Zodiac Family, 102

Betsy Kenoff-Boyd doesn't usually do word-limit poems or like following rules. She lives in Redondo Beach with her family & teaches ESL, so she must like some rules.
Kid vs. Adult Prayers, 73

Josiah Knox
Cold Sparkling Water, 157

Lily Krol is 7 ½ years old and loves to write!
Watching, Wondering, Waiting, Why?, 128

Micah Kunkle is a 15 year old filmmaker who has his own YouTube Channel, Micahproductions. In his free time he enjoys playing with friends, building Legos, reading, surfing, and playing Minecraft. He has a passion for writing Science Fiction and Mysteries.
A Day, 50
Music, Film, Rhyme, 161

Paige Kunkle
Dear Cut Up Pineapple, 155

Lilith Lanier
The Trouble With Sisters, 119

Robert Little Lanphar Jr.: LilBob has excelled at athletics, science & engineering, volunteerism, family life and is now trying to become a poet.
St. Denis Corridor of Lights, 120
Redondo Beach in Shroud, 140

Sophia Larsen lives in Tustin, CA with her parents, Scot and Yumi. She loves to read, play Minecraft, and hang with her friends.
Ten is Approaching, 65
Horses, 135

Eric Lawson is a writer, actor, and producer living in the never dull city of Inglewood. He is the author of several humor books, poetry chapbooks, and short films. He is most proud of his amazing daughter, Amy.
Autumn Hue, 45
The Rose Near Broadway & 3rd, 86

Marie Lecrivain is the editor of The Whiteside Review: A Journal of Speculative/Science Fiction, a Pushcart Prize nominee, and writer-in-residence in her apartment. She's the author of several works of poetry and fiction, including The Virtual Tablet of Irma Tre (© 2014 Edgar & Lenore›s Publishing House), and Grimm Conversations (© 2015 Sybaritic Press).
"i can't even…", 30
The Difference Between, 162

Mike Lemp, Age 73, Lake Forest, CA. Retired. Love to write, hate to proof read!
Love Potion, 88
What is it?, 200

Gerald Locklin has published thousands of short poems and too many long ones. He apologizes for the latter.
Long Shot Double-Sequel, 184

MJ: Front man of MJ and the Space Jams. Never submitted anything like this before!
"A Simple Smile", 99

Maggie Magana is 12 years old and loves to read. She wrote this poem remembering her grandmother's silly cat.
There Once Was a Cat Named Pat, 137

Betsy Mars is a Connecticut-born longtime resident of Southern California, and a lover of language, animals, travel, and even some people. She is grateful for the support she has gotten for her written work from Raundi as well as many others. Currently in a period of exploration and transition, she is excited to see what the future brings.
Apple Picking, 46
Black Hole, 78

Matthew Matusiewicz is a sixteen-year-old sophomore studying creative writing at the Orange County School of the Arts in Santa Ana, California. He hopes to end the era of social inequality in his lifetime, or at least be a part of the solution.
Sorting the Trash. 38
End Of the Line, 198

Mari Maxwell's work is forthcoming in Veils, Halos and Shackles (Kasva Press, Israel) in April 2016. Her works have been published online and in print publications in the USA, UK, Brazil and India. And in case you haven't guessed: She lives in Connemara, Ireland.
My Malaysian Friend, 49
Winter Étude, 141

Ellyn Maybe, Southern California based poet, United States Artist nominee 2012, has performed both nationally and internationally as a solo artist and with her band. Her work has been included in many anthologies and she is the author of numerous books and a critically acclaimed poetry/music album, Rodeo for the Sheepish. Her latest poetry/music project is called Ellyn & Robbie www. ellynmaybe.com
Enjoy the World!, 1
He's a Handful, 74
Someday Our Peace Will Come, 201

Terry McCarty has been writing poetry in, around and sometimes about Southern California since 1997. His books/chapbooks include HOLLYWOOD POETRY: 2001-2013, 20 GREATEST HITS and I SAW IT ON TV. Terry was part of last year's ATTACK OF THE POEMS
anthology.
A Visit to the Doctor, 72
Red Wind, 146

Daniel McGinn's poems have appeared numerous anthologies and publications. Daniel has an MFA in writing from Vermont College of Fine Arts. He and his wife, poet Lori McGinn, are natives of Whittier, California.
Almost Eden, 25
Growing up, 66
Man with a Walker, 91

Lori McGinn enjoys writing, baking, painting, hanging out with friends and family, and her happy place is Maui!. She is a wife, homemaker, Mom, Grandma, waitress, and warn many hats through many years. Her favorite color is purple, and favorite activity is swimming.
I Am Not This Person Lost In The Family Tree, 125
Winter Comes knocking on my back door, 142s

Deanne Meeks Brown (aka The Yes Mom) is currently pursuing her Master's Degree in Clinical Counseling and Psychology in a magical place Allen Ginsberg once called, "the center of the universe" and Bernie Sander's utilized as his hub for social activism - Goddard College in Plainfield, Vermont. Like Bernie, Deanne dreams of a world where everyone has access to the cookie jar.
Open, 34

Neela Michelsen
Room of Curly Singers, 151

Briannah Milne:
Bravery, 147
Pineapple, 154

Erin Milne is in 8th Grade and has been writing poems for as long as she remembers. Her main inspiration is her mother, and the ups and downs of life. Erin's favorite poet of all time is Dr. Seuss.
Hope, 131
The Grass is Greener on the Other Side, 190

Aryanna Miramontes is a 4th grader who has been published before, loves to try new things.
If Bubbles Were Bullets, 56
The Regret Ride, 61

Kaleb Moniz is 13 years old and lives in Irvine California. He has one brother and two sisters. He enjoys playing soccer and video games.
Pizza, 158

Carter Moon was born in the foothills of the Rocky Mountains of Colorado. He made his way out West to pursue dreams, cats, and the occasional woman. You can find him on xfdrmag.net.
The Signal is Dying, 129
Electric Ruination, 199

Ralph R. Moore is an astrologer, writer, and father of seven. He is the developer of Base Frames and the TRUSA (The True Horoscope of The United States) A.skysearch.net
The Illusive Factor, 87

Raundi K. Moore-Kondo is a writer, publisher and musician who founded For The Love of Words Creative Writing Workshop and Small Press. www.theLoveofWords.com
The Last Thing I Want To See Before I Die, 168

Eric Morago is a poet and geek living in Los Angeles. He dreams of being a superhero, but knows from experience spandex chafes. Google him.
Reverse, 12

Victor Morales is a fifth grade student, second time getting published. Great at math, loves and is awesome at baseball.
Scarecrow, 148

Emma Morrison is an animal lover who likes to write.
Sitting, 47
Walking, 132

Jacob Munoz likes too many topics to fit into 1 sentence, but he likes soccer.
Death By Rhyme, 186

Annie Neal is a 9 year old 4th grader who attends the CHEP homeschool program. She loves gymnastics, art, Star Wars and bacon. She is grateful for Miss Raundi's Creative Writing class as it gives her an opportunity to express herself.
My Favorite Fairytale Is, 144

Dani Neiley is an assistant editor at Drunk Monkeys and Editor-in-Chief of Calliope, Chapman University's art and literary magazine. Her work has been published in Calliope, Bartleby Snopes, Green Blotter, and Polaris.
benign, 35

Glen Nesbitt lives in Long Beach with his beautiful cat and even more beautiful no kids.
Soap, 55
Forever, 93
10 Hot Teachers, 197

Richard Nester is the featured poet in the Summer 2015 issue of Floyd County Moonshine. His book Buffalo Laughter was published by Alabaster Leaves Press in 2014.
What One Gets Eventually, 44

Robbi Nester remembers what it was like to be a kid and has written about it frequently. You can find some of these poems in her book, A Likely Story (Moon Tide, 2014). More such poems will appear in her forthcoming collection, Other-Wise, which will be published sometime in 2016 by Tebot Bach Press.
Tree Frog: A Self-Portrait, 9
Under the Ironing Machine, 68
Seal, 134

David Ohlsen tries his best to be a nice guy. He's in graduate school at CSULB, has published a few poems before, and he hopes you're having a nice day :-)
I Wanna Be a Space Detective, 110
I Wanna Be a Judge, 175
I Wanna Be a Writer, 182

Mark Olague is an a full-time instructor at Cerritos Community College. He currently lives with his wife in Seal Beach, CA.
Nightmarch, 3
Object Study, 77

James Palacio: Google Jaimes Palacio! He has written for periodicals, hosted and booked award winning readings like PENGUINS HOOKED ON MACARONICS and has appeared in numerous antholigies including A POET IS A POET NO MATTER HOW TALL, ATTACK OF THE PO-EMS! and a POET'S HAGGADAH. (even though he is not Jewish!) His chapbooks for sale are now all out of print. He is baffled to discover he has become one of the two most requested disc jockeys (his day job) at FLY BY NIGHT. Kristen Stewart once liked his poems.
Possible, 23
Self Portrait in Charcoal, 32
My First Poem of the Night, 189

Alan Passman writes poetry amongst other forms of verse and prose. He is also an educator, a musician, a cat dad, a husband, and is stuck between Gen X and the Millennials.
Bemoaning, 152
Scrawled on a Box in my Closet, 188

Cynthia Quevedo is the wife of a man who keeps her laughing, the mother of three fabulous people and a relunctant New England transplant. She is very proud to have her poems published in A Poet is a Poet No Matter How Tall; Episode II: Attack of the Poems; Lummox Number Four 2015; and Fire in the Tree-tops, 2015 HNA Anthology.
Blast of Spring, 27
Rain, 28

Lydia Quevedo is a high school senior from rural VT who discovered her passion for writing when she was seven, and has written her way well across space and time ever since. When not schooling, she works on her novels, acts, sings, knits, plays piano and tennis (not simultaneously), obsessively raises tomatoes, and learns foreign languages. Previously her work has appeared in A Poet Is A Poet No Matter How Tall and on her somewhat erratically curated blog, as well as through the mic at poetry slams. She thanks her poetry mentor for encouraging a little spark of creativity to grow into a happy inferno.
Nocturn, 101

Lisa Ramirez is a 5th grader who has been published in The Quest for Puma Poetry, she loves animals and helping people. She also loves sports like football.
The Walking Dead, 166

Raquel Reyes-Lopez: Some almost 22 year old Hispanic Gemini who kisses the moon before she falls asleep. She also has a deep love for poetry. Follow her at raquelreyeslopez.com
If No Saint Appears, 126

Megan Richtman is a bright-eyed freshman at the University of California Davis. While dedicated to the biological sciences, she incorporates her love for the natural world into her paintings and poems whenever possible. Other interests include obsessively geeking out over movies and being an extreme cat enthusiast. Seriously, cats are radical.
The Ancient Whale, 17
Field of Gravestone, 127

Cindy Rinne creates art and writes in San Bernardino, CA. She brings myth to life in contemporary context. Cindy is the author of spider with wings (Jamii Publishing), Quiet Lantern is forthcoming (Turning Point), Breathe in Daisy, Breathe out Stones is forthcoming (FutureCycle Press), and she co-authoredSpeaking Through Sediment with Michael Cooper (ELJ Publications). www.fiberverse.com.
Today I Got Invited To Visit India, 51
Spirals, 104

Vaughan Risher: There's never been a moment where Vaughan didn't question the value of being a "jack of all trades", but that's what he is.
Epiphany, 84
My Shark, 179

Robert Rodriguez is a published Los Angeles poet who has been lagging on writing. His intentions are to write every day but you know the cliché, "life happens". Well, it does. Which means his pens have collected more dust than fingerprints lately.
Visual Stimulation, 173

Matt Rouse writes poetry
because that is the only way
the voices in his head make any sense.
Belly Flop, 6
A Useful Thing, 37

Aseah Sabir is 8 ½ and likes drawing, baking with her family and going to many classes.
Pink and White Pillow, 100
I Am a Wonderful Creature, 138

Fatima Shaikh is 8 years old and totally interested in playing sports. She especially loves ice-skating and never wants to miss Tae Kwan Do. Whenever she sees a book she can't leave until she reads it.
Nature's Flowers, 85

Ayaan Sheikh is almost 10 years old and likes art, baking and rollerskating.
Cotton Candy, 159

Emaan Sheikh likes roller-blading, playing soccer, swim class, making snow-girls in winter and art.
My Toy Penguin, 71

Linda Singer has been published poetry in several journals including Lummox 2, 3, and 4, Directions, Spring Harvest, and The Moment. Three of her one acts plays have been produced in Dallas, Texas and her chapbook, *Vital Signs* is currently available.
Summer 2015, 52
Then There Was, 90

Graham Smith is a
bar napkin haikuist
living in long beach
taking baby steps, 79
he turned on the lights, 82
four valentines, 139

Clifton Snider has been writing poems since he was in the sixth grade. His latest book of poems is Moonman: New and Selected Poems (World Parade Books, 2012). His fourth novel, The Plymouth Papers, was published by Spout Hill Press in 2014.
The Now, or Nothing at All, 107
No Worries, 108

Ellie Sommer is a fourteen year old un-socialized homeschooler who hopes to one day take over the planet (or at least write about someone who does).
At The Little Corner Pet Shop, 164

Alexis Tan is a 13 year old girl who loves to draw, read, and write. She enjoys writing both novels and short poems. She has written two novels and is hoping to finish her third... Someday. Alexis also has a passion for good stories, so she often reads all sorts of books. In her free time, she draws animals and other things that interest her.
Caged, 15
Teddy Bear, 70

Thomas R. Thomas
writes very short poems
succinctly
Touch the pages, 43
This Moment, 176

Jeri Thompson: Funny story, although she prefers poems that are short, she has very few short, short poems. A resident of Long Beach for twenty five years (OC transplant). Her poetry has appeared in Mas Tequila Review, RedLightLit and soon to appear in Chiron. Things are good.
Working Out, 96

Ben Trigg is the co-host of Two Idiots Peddling Poetry at the Ugly Mug in Orange, California. When all else fails, Ben goes to Disneyland.
The Fire Dodging Chemist Burns Popcorn, 185
If You Ask a Poet to Do Math, 196

Aaron Vega
Recipe for a Monkey Taco, 170

Moira Ward is 13 and known as Artisticly-Anonymous on Deviant Art. She enjoys writing poetry and short stories and has participated in NaNoWriMo (National Novel Writing Month,) twice, and has completed the fifty thousand word goal both times. She hopes to one day publish a novel of her very own.
Thinking, 122

Y.K. Watts: Yeggi Kaela Watts is a proud mommy and Behavior Therapist living in the Long Beach Community. Most of her free time is spent singing, songwriting, painting and writing poetry in hopes of connecting with people from all walks of life.
Reflection, 112

Ellen Webre is a California poet with a taste for the eerie and supernatural. The fingers of dreams bring strange visions, and the world brings the language to express them. She is in her last year of college and will be off to bring the world even more strangeness and delight.
Alligator Girl, 5
Headdress, 149

Naomi Ke'aloha Williams is eight years old. She loves writing. Especially writing poems.
The Bird is Beautiful, 191

A.D. Winans is a native San Francisco award-winning poet. His work has been published worldwide and translated into eight languages. He is the former editor and publisher of Second Coming and is on the advisory board of the New York Quarterly.
Rain Poem, 26
Li Po, 29

Natalie Yee is currently a sophomore at St. Margaret's Episcopal School. She has enjoyed writing poetry all her life and has received several awards from the Scholastic Art and Writing Competition for her poems. Her other passions in life includes piano, golf, and volunteering in the Math for Service organization.

Waves, 105
Without Knowing, 163

Rebekah Yospe is 15 and loves animals. Especially skunk, raccoons, pandas and opossums. She also really loves her friends and tacos.

Vampires, 113